FRANK LLOYD WRIGHT TRUST

THE OAK PARK HOME AND STUDIO OF
FRANK LLOYD WRIGHT

WRITTEN BY ANN ABERNATHY   DESIGNED BY JOHN G. THORPE

FRANK LLOYD WRIGHT lived and worked in Oak Park from 1889 until 1909. He raised six children with his first wife, Catherine, in the home and began his remarkable seventy-year career in the adjacent studio. Here Wright created a wholly new form of American architecture known as the Prairie style because it reflects the landscape of the midwestern plains. Through frequent additions and modifications, Wright's Oak Park home and studio served as the first testing ground for his imaginative genius. A tour of the building moves from the early home to the later studio, a sequence that reveals the evolving ideas of his first twenty years in practice and the origin of the principles he was to develop throughout the rest of his career.

ORIGINAL HOME, 1889

PLAYROOM ADDITION, 1895

STUDIO ADDITION, 1898

GARAGE ADDITION, 1911

CHICAGO AVENUE

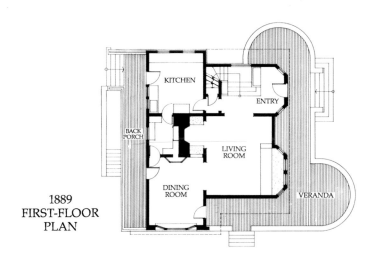

West facade

1889
FIRST-FLOOR
PLAN

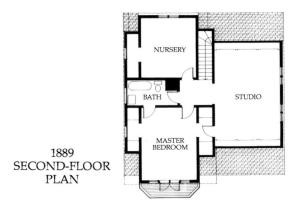

1889
SECOND-FLOOR
PLAN

FRANK LLOYD WRIGHT was born in 1867 in Richland Center, Wisconsin. His father was William Carey Wright, a well-respected but restless minister and music master; his mother was Anna Lloyd-Jones Wright, a strong-willed schoolteacher. The family moved several times, to small parishes in Iowa, Rhode Island, and Massachusetts, returning to the Madison area in 1878. Anna was an active influence on her son: she hung engravings of cathedrals in the nursery and gave him lessons in form and design using the Froebel "gifts" —sets of wooden blocks, strips of paper, and gridded sheets that made learning about geometry a tactile experience. "All are in my fingers to this day," Wright always claimed.

In summers he labored on the nearby farms of his Welsh, Unitarian uncles. He later said, "The book of creation is my textbook," a creed he absorbed from the rolling hills of Wisconsin. Wright discounted the importance of his formal schooling, and after only two semesters of engineering he left college abruptly in 1887 to seek employment in Chicago.

Wright's first job was with Joseph Lyman Silsbee, a prominent architect known for picturesque Shingle-style buildings. This style is characterized by smooth, swelling volumes, shingled surfaces, broad low proportions, and asymmetrical plans—all traits that can be seen in Wright's Oak Park home.

Wright was profoundly influenced by the work of his next employers, Louis Sullivan and Dankmar Adler. Sullivan, famous for his ornament inspired by nature, crusaded for an authentic American architecture based on the principle that a building's form should honestly follow its function. Hired originally to develop detailed sketches for the Auditorium Building, Wright rose quickly to the position of head draftsman and developed remarkable skill in residential architecture.

In 1889, Sullivan loaned Wright the money to buy a lot and build a home in Oak Park for himself and his bride-to-be, Catherine Tobin. He was twenty-one; she was eighteen.

The first-floor plan of the new house shows a compact group of rooms neatly arranged around a central chimney core. The wide openings from the entry to the living room and from there to the dining room create a diagonal movement, with views out to the west and north yards. The living room bay protrudes into the expansive veranda. Wright was beginning to break the rigid shape of rooms, opening them up and allowing them to flow freely, one into another. On the other side of the chimney core, the kitchen and pantry are contained rooms facing south and east to the back porch.

The second-floor plan of 1889 is also compact and has a minimum of hallway. The bath, stairhall, and closet acted as sound buffers between the bedrooms. The east side of the second floor, including the closets and part of the bath, is cantilevered out over the first floor wall as shelter for the back porch. The master bedroom has a

Frank Lloyd Wright,
a self-portrait, in 1904

Catherine Tobin Wright,
in 1908

1895
FIRST-FLOOR
PLAN

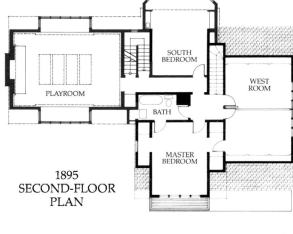

1895
SECOND-FLOOR
PLAN

balcony on the north. Wright used the west room as a studio for his after-hours work.

NEEDING MONEY for his new family but also to fulfill his personal drive for architectural expression, Wright designed several houses secretly, violating the terms of his contract with Sullivan. This resulted in an angry parting in 1893, and Wright opened his own office in downtown Chicago.

Wright's family grew as quickly as his practice. The little house on Forest Avenue overflowed with six children: Lloyd was born in 1890, John in 1892, Catherine in 1894, David in 1895, Frances in 1898, and Robert Llewellyn in 1903. Wright added an east wing in 1895, providing a new kitchen and maid's room and, upstairs, a large playroom. The old kitchen was expanded and became the new dining room. At about the same time, the second bay window was added in the living room, forming a double wrap-around bay with a generous view.

Upstairs Wright divided the west room with a partition so that the north space became a bedroom for the boys, the south for the girls. The former nursery became Catherine's dayroom. The large barrel-vaulted playroom, a structural tour de force, was a gymnasium, kindergarten, concert hall, and theater all in one.

With these additions the original plan had grown appendages in several directions and became clearly cross-axial, a prototype for the great Prairie homes to emerge in the following decade.

Wright decorated the early interiors of the home in an eclectic manner familiar in the 1890s, including Greek sculpture, *kakemono* (Japanese paintings on silk), oriental rugs, a Chinese stool, and Jacobean chest, along with some built-in cabinets and benches. The whole was lit by Victorian lamps. Brocaded cloth and velvet portieres added texture, and corners were softened with showy plants. Very soon, Wright would opt for decorative arts and furniture that he designed to match his architecture.

Living room

Rendering of north facade

IN 1898, WRIGHT moved his five-year-old architectural practice to Oak Park, attaching a studio workplace to his home. The village was a rapidly developing suburb that provided him many commissions for residences. He felt that a semi-rural setting would be more conducive to creativity than downtown Chicago. Most important was his desire to bring the two aspects of his life—work and family—closer together. Wright worked long hours, and he needed the comforts of home as much as his family needed his presence. This close relationship between home and work was a pattern he was to follow for the rest of his life.

Talented young apprentices, inspired by his mission of reforming architecture, came to work for Wright. They emulated him even in their dress—long hair, soft ties, and smocks. Working endless hours for a common purpose led by the studio master, they became a work family, nurtured by the beauty all around them. The ambience of the studio released each individual's creativity. Marion Mahoney, Walter Burley Griffin, Francis Barry Byrne, William Drummond, and John Van Bergen were among his protégés.

Wright felt that buildings should reflect their natural setting, enhance the character of materials, function according to human needs, and speak to the human soul. The Prairie style, developed during the Oak Park years, was the first real step in the progression toward Wright's organic principles. In this studio, he completed approximately 125 buildings, a quarter of his life's work, in just eleven years. Such masterpieces as the Willits, Thomas, Dana, Darwin Martin, Robie, Coonley, and Gale houses epitomize the residences he designed here, both high budget and low. Among the public structures designed during this period were the Larkin Administration, an office building with a multistory atrium, and Unity Temple, a church of monolithic reinforced concrete.

The studio itself exhibits the Prairie style principles practiced within it. In the early rendering of the facade the most striking feature is the grouping of three geometric solids. The central rectangle connects two octagonal drums, pure idealized forms that display the Prairie style aesthetic: The elements are arranged asymmetrically; they are united through a weaving of window shapes, pilasters, and horizontal bands; the facade is rusticated by the texture of shingle, board and batten, and brick and stone; the broad brick wainscot is a heavy base that roots the building to the ground and connects it to the home; fences reach out to the limits of the site, incorporating the wooded setting; and vegetation is interspersed with the building in urns, planting beds, and a magnificent backdrop of ginkgo and willow trees. The building is in harmony with the land rather than a discordant order imposed by man.

By 1909, Wright had changed the diamond panes to a rectilinear art glass pattern, the peaked roofs to flat ones, and the open entry to a less direct approach in order to discourage curiosity seekers and to enrich the experience of entering.

Drafting room

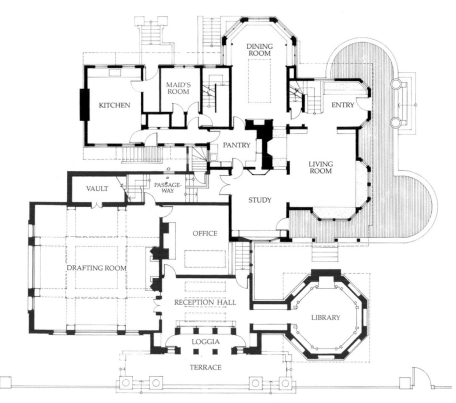

**1898–1909
FIRST-FLOOR
PLAN**

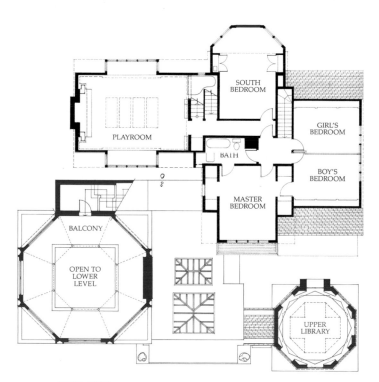

**1898–1909
SECOND-FLOOR
PLAN**

At last, work was along side home . . . the young architect's studio workshop was on Chicago Avenue, the young mother's home and kindergarten continued, still kept growing on Forest Avenue . . . a double-barreled establishment.

THE STUDIO fills almost all of the north yard of the home; its business entrance faces directly on Chicago Avenue. The reception hall links two major spaces —the drafting room and the library. Wright's own office opened to both the reception hall and the drafting room.

The open plan of the drafting room allows for multiple use. The studio spaces are divided by glass doors and the great fireplace mass, a central hearth around which activity flowed, as in the home. In the drafting room, work stations for up to eight draftsmen are defined only by furniture. There are no columns or cubicles.

In marked contrast the octagonal library, or conference room, is isolated and formal, as its use dictated. The two ends of the building, drafting room and library, are similar in their solid lower walls, octagon shape, high windows, spaces focused inward, and light coming from above.

Wright built the passageway between the home and studio around a willow tree rather than sacrifice it to his plan.

*The house began to associate
with the ground and become natural
to its prairie site.*

THE WOODED CORNER LOT that Wright selected was
once the nursery of a Scottish landscape gardener and
had profuse native and exotic plantings. Wright's was
one of the early homes on Forest Avenue, which had
only recently been paved. There were few buildings on
Chicago Avenue, and so the view north was to the
prairie. Wright located the house at the south edge of
the lot, maximizing the view of the luxuriant site and
perhaps also anticipating the day when Chicago Avenue
might become a busy thoroughfare.

On the front of the home deep shadows accentuate
the shapes of the great triangular gable, the octagonal
bays, and circular veranda. The surfaces reveal their
underlying forms with an honesty, almost austerity, not
found in the "bedevilled box" of Victorian homes.
Details are also composed of primary shapes—rectangu-
lar bands of windows, rows of dentils, diamond panes,
and sawtoothed shingles as well as the lunette window
under the peak of the roof.

Wright took the primary symbol of a home, the
sheltering roof, and brought it down low. The solid
veranda wall rises up naturally from the ground. In
between, the first floor is a narrow, well-protected band,
its wall undulating in and out of the shadows cast by
the eaves. It seems to offer little support to the huge
roof hovering above.

Garden walls extend to the edges of the lot, anchor-
ing the home to its site. The entire building fits into its
natural surroundings, nestling down under the trees
and growing up out of the ground. A natural tapestry is
woven with the earth-brown shingles, ivy-covered
bricks, and deep green trim repeating the mossy velvet
of the roof shingles. Foliage is everywhere, in the planting beds, lawns, shrubbery, and trees.

The home projects a simple grandeur without losing
the feeling of a homey cottage. The overscaled roof,
wide front door, and grand steps flanked by piers and
flowering urns give the feeling of monumentality without being overbearing. The sweeping veranda, encircled
by masonry walls like rooms under the sky, is a hospit-
able transition to the inside. The entry is unusually
direct for Wright. Later homes are known for hidden,
even mysterious, approaches to the front door.

ABOVE *On the steps of the home in 1890, from left to
right, are Jenkin Lloyd Jones and his wife Susan, Wright's
sister Jane, Catherine holding Lloyd, Wright's mother, his sister
Maginel, Wright, and Mary, his cousin.*

LEFT *The entry to Wright's home is direct and welcoming.
Primary geometric shapes are found in the overall forms
as well as in the details.*

*Repose is the
highest quality in the art
of architecture.*

*This historic photograph provides a view of the early staircase
and living room during the Wrights' residence.*

A HANDCRAFTED STAIRCASE highlights the small foyer. Constructed of quartersawn oak, the stairway introduces to visitors Wright's lifelong affinity for geometric forms. The intersection of vertical and horizontal planes and the use of square spindles, which he favored to create the play of light and shadow, convey a sense of movement typical in Wright's work.

A plaster frieze and cornice ring the upper wall. A copy of the Hellenistic altar of Pergamum from 200 B.C., the frieze depicts a battle of the gods, a dynamic struggle of balance between opposing forces. Wright, at twenty-one, apparently thought these plaster copies appropriate and affordable. Although he railed against the use of Classical forms in contemporary architecture, Wright admired Greek sculpture.

The staircase was restored with the assistance of the architect's son, David Wright, who recalled racing in from the yard with his five young siblings and bounding up the stairs. In winter they paused just long enough on the oak bench to pull off their boots, leaving them to dry on the the hot-air register. The wide landing faces the living room, providing a platform for making a grand entry down the steps to the first floor.

*The fire burning deep in the
masonry of the home gave a warm feeling.
A feeling that came to stay.*

THE ENTRY, LIVING ROOM, AND STUDY (originally the dining room) form a spacious area in combination, yet each functions separately. A musical event in the living room might be observed from the foyer with the entry stair for seating. The study, lined with cabinets full of books for a family of avid readers, is where the children did their homework. In the living room they could curl up with a book on the window seat or in the fireplace niche, called an "inglenook." On the mantel are inscribed Wright's dual, lifelong ideals of individual integrity and fellowship.

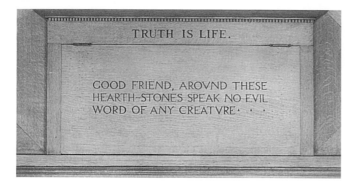

TRUTH IS LIFE.

GOOD FRIEND, AROVND THESE
HEARTH-STONES SPEAK NO EVIL
WORD OF ANY CREATVRE · · ·

The combination of small special places within an open floor area for larger gatherings fit the fluctuating needs of the growing family. With no Victorian sliding doors to exclude children, only soft velours and Japanese hangings separated these rooms, and chains of oriental rugs linked them together.

Delicate wood trim folds around walls, binding all three rooms into a unit. The trim above the door openings increases the sense of spaciousness overhead and also lowers the scale to human height. With the chair rail raised, the trim stratifies the wall into three horizontal bands of color, which unite these spaces.

The first-floor rooms are organized around an inner core, a massing of fireplaces, parts of walls, and built-in furniture. In the middle of this cluster, in the center of the home is the hearth. Formed of materials that come from the ground, it is solid like the earth. Wright organized virtually all the residences he designed around exposed masonry fireplaces.

Above the inglenook seats, there are two openings and above the mantel a false one, actually a mirror. Through these openings the trimwork crisscrosses the inner core, resolving the verticality of the chimney mass and expanding the horizontal space of the living room.

*Wide openings connect the entry, living room,
and study. In the center of the home is the fireplace and
the inglenook seating area.*

"HORIZONTAL LINES, . . . scattered vases filled with leaves and wild flowers, massive fireplaces seemed to be everywhere. Here and there a Yourdes [rug] of rare beauty covered the floor. A Persian lantern, samovars, windows which met and turned corners, lights filtering through fret-sawn ceiling grilles, sunshine and shadows . . . these made the house that was our home."
—John Lloyd Wright

These first-floor spaces create a sense of discovery. In the living room two bays, common in homes of that day, are joined at the corner to form an uncommon wrap-around window that pushes beyond the wall to afford a panoramic view. A precursor of Wright's famous corner windows, these conjoined bays "break the box" of the room. Outswinging windows and overhanging eaves extend the view to the yard beyond.

The view from the study into the living room suggests that the corner bay is the beginning of a larger series of glass panels that continue in the study, where there is a glass door to the veranda and another bay window. Wright called such dissolved walls "light screens." He often quoted a passage from Lao-tzu, the Taoist philosopher: "The reality of the space is not in the walls themselves but in the space contained to be lived in."

Wright's technique of expanding space from a fixed, solid core and dissolving the outer edge was prophetic. Developed further in his Prairie style years, it reached ultimate expression in the Kaufmann house, Fallingwater, forty-six years later. Although very early, this area of the home is in a sense one of the most modern.

ABOVE *A view of the living room from the study shows an expanse of diamond-paned glass.*

ABOVE LEFT *The living room wrap-around bay window above the built-in seats.*

My sense of "wall" was no longer the side of a box. It was enclosure of space affording protection against storm or heat only when needed. But it was also to bring the outside world into the house and let the inside of the house go outside. In this sense I was working away at the wall as a wall and bringing it toward the function of a screen.

*It is the first great principle
of any growth that the thing be no mere
aggregation. Integration means no
part of anything is of any great value
in itself except as it be an integrate
part of the harmonious whole.*

ENTRY TO THE DINING ROOM is through a low vestibule under the front stairs, past a green velvet portiere. The intimate repose of the dining room contrasts markedly with the free and open spaces of the living room seen through an interior opening. To the left is the dark terra cotta mass of the tiled fireplace projecting from the central chimney core, and just beyond that the doorway to the pantry.

The family of eight was often joined for dinner by special guests—clients, artists, writers, and other visitors from around the world. Catherine was an engaging hostess, Frank displayed wit and panache, and such festive occasions gave their house the air of a "jolly carnival," according to John.

The dining room (originally the kitchen) was completely remodeled in 1895. Wright extended the space to the south by adding an octagonal bay. He took this opportunity to create an integrated design in which all elements—exterior shell, windows, interior finishes, recessed lighting, concealed heating, and furniture —were designed together. The large oak table in the center of the room is lit by soft light from the fretwork ceiling grille. Bounded by high-backed, spindled chairs, the dining room furniture defines a "room within a room."

The original ceiling was lowered to accommodate the ceiling grille, probably the first example of recessed lighting. This low ceiling plane and the high baseboard band create a cave-like closeness in the room that is relieved by the bright open bay end. The vista is enriched by art objects and lotus-patterned glass in the bay. Like those in the living room, the bay here has been made to serve other uses—shelves, counters, and radiator enclosures. The architecture incorporates furniture and the furniture is architectural.

Wright deemphasized the junctures of the walls and ceiling, merging them into what he called a "plasticity of form," which created continuity between the elements of the room. Here the ceiling fabric folds down the walls, and the floor tiles run up the fireplace wall.

Simple grace is achieved by the use of humble materials—oak, painter's flax, hearth tiles—left natural or lightly stained to enhance the grain and earth tones. Many materials and textures combine to produce a homogeneous visual richness—a radical departure from the ornateness of contemporary Victorian homes.

ABOVE *The dining room hearth and floor are covered with red clay tiles. Warm earth colors characterize this room.*

OPPOSITE *The dining table and chairs form a "room within a room." Light from the art glass bay windows at the end of the room contrasts with the dark interior.*

BELOW *The pattern of the ceiling grille represents stylized oak tree branches and leaves. This is the first use of recessed, indirect lighting.*

THE PANTRY dates from 1889, when it was located between the original kitchen and the original dining room. A window in the back of the china cabinet allowed a server to get dishes without disturbing the guests. The pantry was enlarged in 1895 and a sink added. Wright included generous cabinet and drawer space for glassware and linens.

The 1895 kitchen was the domain of the maid who did the cooking. The children were scolded for using the back door and running through her kitchen, but they had fond memories of making taffy and fudge during holiday preparations. The cast iron stove, stoked with wood or coal, generated a lot of heat. Four large casement windows and the open high ceiling provided cross-ventilation and light.

Kitchen access was through the south yard, where coal and ice were delivered. Along the driveway were the chicken coops and wire runways, where David raised pigeons. The children had ponies in the shed at the end of the driveway. Wright stabled his horse across Forest Avenue and later parked his sporty yellow Stoddard Dayton roadster at the curb.

A delightful, somewhat random pattern of openings animates the south facade. A series of art glass panels wraps around the dining room bay; high above is the long rectangle of the south bedroom clerestory; the green-gold playroom bay is cantilevered out from the wall, sheltering the back porch. In Wright's hands even this backyard facade becomes a lively composition.

ABOVE *The pantry*

ABOVE LEFT *The 1895 kitchen was the domain of the maid.*

OPPOSITE *The south drive was a utilitarian area but the facade is a handsome composition.*

TOP *The mural on the south wall depicts an American plains Indian figure.*

———

ABOVE *The stencil pattern of the upper wall matches one in Sullivan's Auditorium Building.*

———

BELOW RIGHT *The window of the master bedroom from the exterior.*

———

OPPOSITE *The master bedroom, looking north. The high ceiling gives a spacious feeling to a small room.*

Architecture speaks as poetry to the soul.

THE MASTER BEDROOM is an opulent private sanctum that expands with an upward sweep into what Wright considered the useless space of the attic. The vaulted ceiling, suggesting a sky-canopy, lends an air of spaciousness to the room. Reinforcing this feeling are the two upper end walls, where there are murals showing wide arches of sky. Painted by Orlando Giannini, the murals depict Indians of the midwestern plains. The birth of a new Americanism was a popular theme of that day, especially with Wright. On the north wall, however, the figure wears a robe of a decidedly Egyptian appearance, and on either side of him, within the room, are amphora-shaped lamps hanging from gilt plaster medallions with a papyrus motif and loops of chains. The lamps almost appear to be part of the painting, and the figure seems to step out below the horizon line onto the shelf underneath. Soft light from the hand-blown opalescent glass shimmers on the golden mural borders. The stencil patterns that ring the upper wall match ones that Sullivan used in the Auditorium Theatre. The birch trim imposes a rational order on this vault. The massive birch bed was designed by Wright.

Under the painted vista of the north mural there is a natural vista through the T-shaped window. The six sashes offer various possibilities for view and ventilation. The lower sash gave access to the balcony, where Catherine rocked the babies before the studio was built.

The bathroom, lined with board and batten oak paneling, served the family of eight.

INDOOR BATHROOMS were still uncommon in 1889. The handsome wall treatment in this one is unusual: horizontal board and batten in quarter-sawn oak, used here in extravagant quantity. The floors are maple and the upper walls are covered with a natural oatmeal paper. The fixtures are typical of the era, all exposed fittings gleaming with the soft luster of nickel plating. Because the original bathroom window looked directly into the playroom that was added in 1895, Wright projected a small bay out and turned the window 90 degrees so that light and air could enter without compromising privacy.

THE WEST ROOM, which served as Wright's studio, fills the space of the great western gable. The high gambrel ceiling shape recalls the Wisconsin barns of Wright's youth. Its rhythmic ceiling trim amplifies the space and defines the inner structure of rafters. Seated at his drafting table, Wright had a view to the west through the broad band of windows.

Around 1895 the need for additional bedroom space prevailed and a six-foot-high partition was added. The boys slept on the north side, the girls on the south, all on folding metal-spring cots. Three shallow closets with honey-colored oak fronts line the side wall of each space. Horizontal oak moldings connect them with the window and door heads and the partition. As the trim turns corners, the plaster walls seem to blend together, emphasizing a continuous surface that Wright called "the folded plane." Below the molding, the wall is

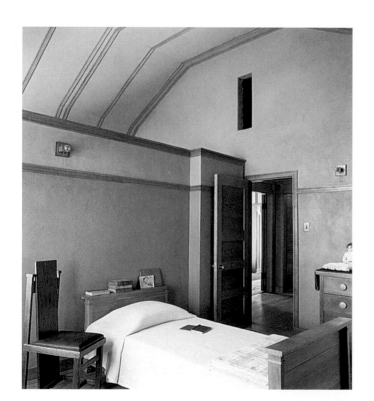

A low wall divided the children's bedroom, girls on the left and boys on the right.

painted dark olive green. Above the partition, the openness of the light green vaulted ceiling is shared by both rooms. The partition was high enough for visual privacy but low enough to allow pillow fights. The high open vault relieves the small bedrooms from a sense of boxy confinement and also contributes to good ventilation on hot summer nights. Wright's accomplishment was to put the children in a minimal space while making them feel they had a big bedroom.

THE SOUTH BEDROOM was Catherine's dayroom, where she read and sketched and sometimes cared for sick children. Abundant light and a serene atmosphere fostered these activities.

The two-level ceiling subtly differentiates subspaces within the room. The south bay, under a low soffit, has strong light and breezes from large outswinging casement windows; the built-in radiator enclosure provides convenient shelf space. The main part of the room has a higher ceiling. Soft light from the yellow glazing in the clerestory window penetrates all the way back into the room. The two natural light sources, reflecting on creamy white wall fabric, provide a uniform luminous glow on sunny days, a bright feeling even on cloudy ones. Catherine's room had a delicacy found nowhere else in the home.

ABOVE *The south bedroom has an upper window to allow light farther back into the room.*

BELOW *Catherine Wright, about 1895, reading to Lloyd and John. Daughter Catherine was in the Tobin family spool crib. David was born later that year.*

Dignified as a tree in the midst of nature but a child of the spirit of man.

EVERYTHING WRIGHT could do architecturally he did in the playroom—the spatial dynamics, functional considerations, illusion, visual metaphor, decorative arts, structural experiment; such variety was characteristic of his early work. The architecture delights the senses and inspires the imagination. *Nature*—water, sky, plants, earth—and *spirit*—freedom, curiosity, hope, wisdom—are for the children to enjoy.

The playroom ceiling is a great barrel vault. It is a clear span of 18 feet: a child could toss a ball in its arc. For six children who spent the long cold season indoors, this was a gymnasium and winter garden. In summer light filters through myriad leaves, as if this were a glade in the woods.

Oak trim branches up to the decorative skylight, which is edged in green. The grille is fretsawed plywood in a geometric pattern of prickly ash leaves and pods. A continuous shelf at the springline conceals the connection of the arch to the wall, making the vault

ABOVE *The narrow hall to the playroom has an arched ceiling that frames the view of the fisherman depicted in the mural above the fireplace.*

OVERLEAF *The playroom looking east shows the 15-foot-high barrel vault.*

OPPOSITE *The gallery at the west end makes the room appear longer than it really is.*

seem unsupported, a triumph over gravity. Because the top of the brick wall is low, scaled for children, the ceiling seems higher.

Inspired by a tale from the Arabian Nights, the mural of the fisherman and the genie over the fireplace was painted by Chicago artist Charles Corwin. The semicircle of sky reinforces the weightless feel of the ceiling vault, and the perspective of the scene carries the eye far beyond the wall plane.

Extending the view at the other end of the room is a gallery, where the barrel vault takes over the attic space of Catherine's dayroom. The graduated heights of the spindled railings create a forced perspective, making the gallery seem much deeper than it is. From its shadows emerges the Winged Victory of Samothrace. A curtain was hung in front of the fireplace to make a stage, and the children charged admission for gallery seats at their theatrical productions.

A grand piano was inserted into the wall under the gallery stairs, suspended by an iron strap. The treads and landing are hinged to open, allowing the sound to escape. Music was an abiding interest throughout Wright's life and the children all played musical instruments. Sound reverberated in the playroom during family musicales, Lloyd conducting with the bow of his cello.

Dualities create drama in Wright's architecture. In the playroom, for example, the heaviness of the dark speckled Roman brick (a truly child-proof material) contrasts with the lightness of the smooth plaster ceiling vault. The room can still seem cozy and warm even though it is large and open.

The playroom expands on each side into window bays that project out beyond the shell of the building. Art glass windows surrounding the built-in toy benches bring in low winter light. They form a transparent screen of abstracted leaves, mingling with the real ones just outside. Thus, the experience is surely one of being perched high in a treehouse with light and leaves on both sides.

The playroom space flows in five directions—out the side windows, into both the mural vista and the gallery, and up through the skylight overhead.

Geometric shapes are found everywhere—the vault, its arches, the ceiling grille. The crossed rectangles of the plan give order to the space. Wall sconces assembled of squares and rectangles provided additional light. Patterns for games were marked on the floor for Catherine's kindergarten. Here the Wright children played with the Froebel "gifts" just as their father had, learning to master the geometric forms underlying nature.

This wondrous environment points to Wright's sensitivity to his children and their development. In describing the playroom, John recalled that his father believed "an instinct for the beautiful would be firmly established by a room whose simple beauty and strength are daily factors."

*That primitive sense of shelter
is a quality architecture should
always have.*

THE WEST FACADE, facing Forest Avenue, is composed of
both the front of the home and the octagonal library.
Wright attempted to connect the two parts of the building visually, despite the different functions within. The
pitched roof of the home symbolizes shelter, safety, and
comfort for the family. The studio is a sturdier-looking
building with flat roofs and a strong weaving of verticals
and horizontals, more self-contained and focused on
the work inside. And Wright diminished the differences
between them to achieve a unified whole.

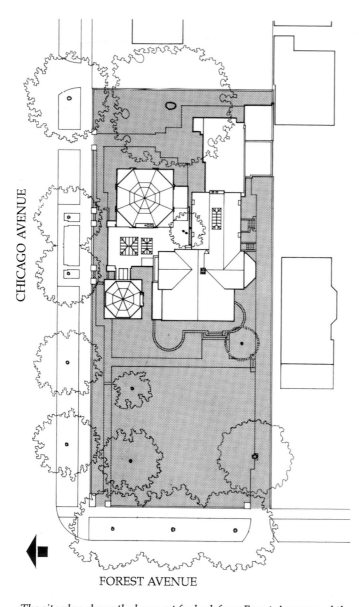

*The site plan shows the home set far back from Forest Avenue and the
studio built close to the sidewalk on Chicago Avenue.*

The studio from the northeast.

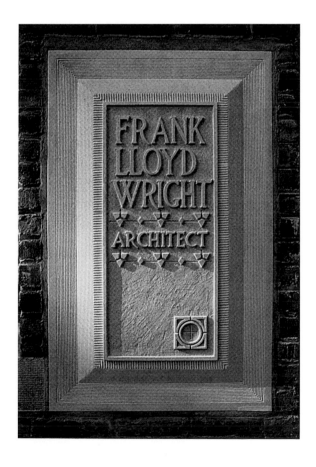

*In architecture,
expressive changes of surface,
emphasis of line, and
especially textures
of materials make facts more eloquent,
forms more significant.*

WHEN WRIGHT BUILT the studio in 1898, he took the opportunity to create a building uniquely suited to an architectural office and to advertise his radical style. Bold shapes, distinctly stated, expressed the interior spaces on the outside. Horizontal planes repeat the ground line, heavy at the bottom and lighter at the top. The studio fits into its natural setting with its asymmetrical massing and texture of common brick and cedar. It is an irony typical of Wright that a masterpiece of design was composed of such commonplace materials.

On the wall next to the entry Wright proudly installed a limestone plaque stating his name and business in hand-hewn letters. The logo at the corner is a cross within a circle within a square. The circle represents the infinite, the square represents integrity and tangibility —a fitting symbol for an architect, the infinite becoming concrete.

The array of arts is impressive. Limestone urns full of flowering plants loom above the steps. Their design is like the logo—a circular form on cross struts over a square base. The entry loggia columns are capped by plaster castings the color of bronze. The whimsical design incorporates Wright's personal symbolism. The book of knowledge issues from the tree of life, a symbol of natural growth. A scroll of architectural plans unrolls from it. On either side are sentry storks, perhaps symbols of wisdom and fertility. The stork panels were executed by Richard Bock, as were the "Boulder" sculptures on high piers flanking the upper entry wall like bookends. These blocky men represent mankind struggling up from the ground to transcend earthly bonds.

The maze-like entry to the studio contrasts sharply with the frontal directness of the home, built fifteen years earlier. A few steps lead up from the sidewalk level to the terrace behind the low brick wall of the studio entry. The recessed doors and two rows of columns make the exact boundary of the building ambiguous. It takes five turns to move from the sidewalk into the reception hall, making the entry sequence seem much longer than its actual 10 feet.

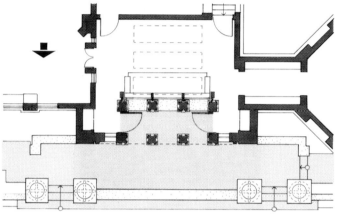

TOP *The studio entrance loggia, with its terrace wall in front.*

ABOVE *Floor plan detail of the terrace loggia and reception hall.*

OPPOSITE *Detail of the studio entry with stork columns, "Boulder" figures, and flowering urns. Decorative arts enhance Wright's best local advertisement— his own workplace.*

BELOW *Textures of limestone trim and rough common brick that Wright used.*

INSIDE THE RECEPTION HALL, it is amazingly quiet compared with noisy Chicago Avenue. This is one of the most mood-evoking areas of the building. The loggia columns with their plaster capitals are seen from inside, their foliage adding permanent greenery to the room. The three art glass skylights are made of myriad green and gold rectangles and clear glass. The natural light coming from these abstractions of leaves adds to the profound calm of this arbor-like room. The reflective gold-painted surface of the walls diminishes the sense of enclosure in a room.

The trim throughout the studio is dark-stained basswood. As in other parts of the building, the trim serves to unify the space. The magnesite flooring is a poured mix of cement, sawdust, and pigment. The oiled finish makes it look like aged leather, but it is very durable.

Along the front wall is a wide plan desk where drawings were spread out for review. Wright said that contractors would sometimes read his name on the drawings, roll up the set, and tell potential clients that they weren't looking for trouble. But, of course, this room helped them see that the effort would be worthwhile.

The reception hall is a link between two important spaces, the octagonal library to the west and the drafting room to the east.

LEFT *The art glass skylight is an abstract pattern inspired by nature.*

OPPOSITE *The studio reception hall is a serene interior with the feel of an outdoor glade. The view beyond is to the octagonal library.*

All things in nature exhibit this tendency to crystallize.

A LOW, DARK HALLWAY like the one to the playroom leads to the octagonal library, where the space expands upward. This exceptional interior, a complex ordering of geometric forms, is more symmetrical and abstract than the reception room. It presages idealized spaces to come, notably the Guggenheim Museum, with its spiral ramp and top light.

The library was used as a conference and presentation room. Lined with books, art objects, and renderings, it displays architectural possibilities in order to intrigue a client. Some of Wright's design practices are presented in this room.

First, the form follows the function. The octagonal form focuses attention inward to the table in the middle, where the architectural plans were laid before clients. No windows at eye level were allowed to distract their gaze. Strong uniform light comes from the high windows and the skylight.

Second, Wright used geometry itself as decorative art, choosing octagons and squares as the basic forms in this room. A hollow crystalline prism, the room is expressed both inside and out. Eight pairs of columns mark the corners between the cabinets. Even the table legs are octagonal. Upper shelves, the ceiling cornices, and skylight frame are all octagonal rings slightly rotated. This skylight is the only one in the building that is devoid of fretwork or art glass. Wright's style reached mature abstraction here.

Third, Wright's lavish use of trim changes the room's proportions. The form is unusually tall, but the library is held to human scale with horizontal layers. All verticals are minimized, even the corner columns, which are capped and banded to be subordinate to the horizontal shelves.

Wright's architecture recalls historical prototypes such as the domed spaces of Europe, but this space is dynamic, creating a spiraling movement upward, toward the light.

ABOVE *Exterior view of the octagonal library shows that the inside form is visible on the outside.*

OPPOSITE *An octagon in floor plan, the shape of the library is repeated upward through shelves and ceiling trim to the skylight.*

BELOW *In this reflected ceiling plan one can see the octagons and squares overlap.*

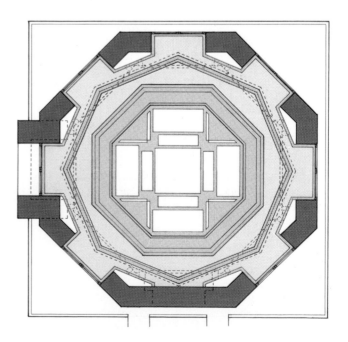

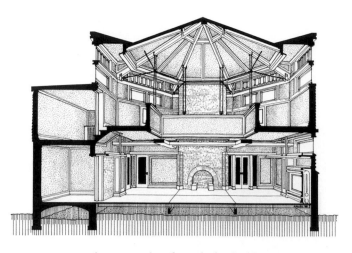

ABOVE *A cross-section through the drafting room shows how the balcony is suspended by chains from the roof beams.*

OPPOSITE *Wright had as many as six apprentice architects working on his Prairie style designs at the first-floor drafting tables. Artists sometimes worked on sculpture and art glass designs on the balcony.*

BELOW *The passageway between the home and the studio was built around a willow tree so that the tree would not have to be cut down.*

THE DRAFTING ROOM, at the opposite end of the reception hall, was the first of Wright's top-lit open-plan workrooms, preceding the Larkin Building (1904) and the Johnson Wax offices (1936). It epitomizes another of Wright's practices: he achieved a unified design through an integration of its parts.

The common-brick walls of the first floor and the arched, buttressed fireplace form the solid core of the studio. Small window areas are on only two sides; Wright wanted his draftsmen to focus attention on their work, not the view. The plaster surfaces continue overhead to form the balcony rail, where sculptors, glass craftsmen, and painters sometimes worked. The upper workspace has far more natural light than the lower; nearly continuous windows give an inspiring view of the treetops.

Vertical supports for the balcony and roof are underplayed. A delicate system of chains rids the space of columns and creates an open plan. The horizontal chains form a tension ring that pulls in on the roof beams and upper walls. This harness eliminates the clutter of cross-ties and allows a clear span above. The chains are a structural solution honestly expressed and a decorative system punctuating the space as well.

The dark-stained wood trim is a system of linear elements both functional and decorative. Ceiling beams emphasize the octagonal shape of the cream-colored dome. The wall trim not only outlines openings but also binds wall planes together. Below the balcony, the trim disengages from the wall to form hanging shelves for models and plants. The shelves also define an invisible horizontal plane and lower the tall proportions of the room. Wright used hanging Holophane spheres for general illumination and green glass shades for focused task lighting.

All furnishings for this room were designed by Wright. The drafting tables have smooth maple tops and dark bases. The draftsmen sat on backless stools. Tall, free-standing cabinets for drawings and supplies divide the workspace.

YE'VE LEFT A GLIMMER STILL TO CHEER
THE MAN—THE ARTIFEX
THAT HOLDS IN SPITE O' KNOCKS AND SCALE
O' FRICTION WASTE AN' SLIP,
AN' BY THAT LIGHT—NOW MARK MY WORD—
WE'LL BUILD THE PERFECT SHIP.

In organic architecture, then,
it is quite impossible to consider
the building as one thing,
its furnishings as another and its
setting still another. . . .
All these work together as one thing.

IN THE FOURTH ROOM, which was Wright's business
office, all the furniture was also designed by Wright.
Plain surfaces are dark-stained basswood and poplar.
The cubelike forms, grouped asymmetrically, divide the
room in the middle and keep the wall spaces clear. The
chairs, designed in 1898, were startlingly modern but of
dubious comfort. Wright himself admitted he was black
and blue from sitting in his own chairs.

At the heart of this room is a fireplace with an arched
opening, again of rough common brick. Strong natural
light from overhead, diffused by etched and colored
glass, gave a work light far superior to artificial illumination. The earth tones in the office, matching the colors
of the rest of the studio, are muted by today's standards
but are sympathetic with the natural beauty Wright
sought to produce. Dried weeds and branches in plain
pottery vases were used for decoration.

ABOVE *These casement windows shine like jewels*
for the passerby at night.

———————

RIGHT *The studio office is bathed in a soft light*
from its skylight.

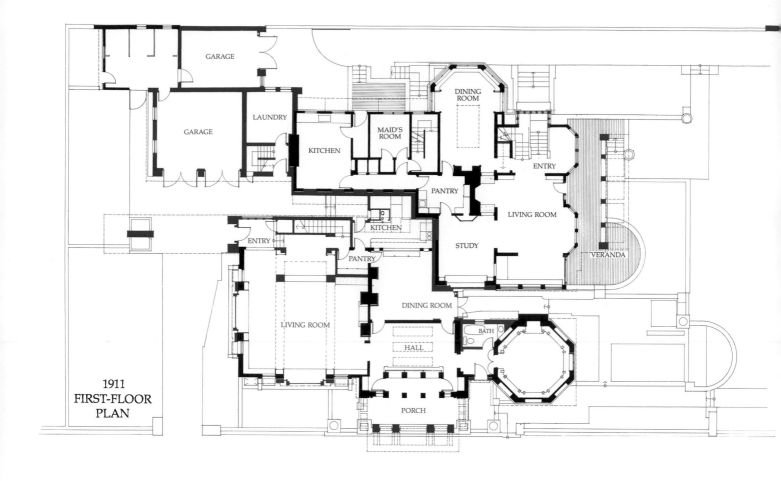

GARAGE

GARAGE

LAUNDRY

KITCHEN

MAID'S ROOM

DINING ROOM

PANTRY

ENTRY

LIVING ROOM

KITCHEN

ENTRY

PANTRY

STUDY

VERANDA

LIVING ROOM

DINING ROOM

BATH

1911
FIRST-FLOOR
PLAN

HALL

PORCH

BY 1909, WRIGHT'S WORK was well publicized nationally but was not universally understood or accepted. The Columbian Exposition of 1893 had revived an interest in classical styles in the United States, but in Europe there were strong movements toward a functional, plain architecture that paralleled Wright's work. In 1909, a German publisher proposed doing a portfolio of Wright's drawings and invited him to come abroad.

Wright welcomed the opportunity to leave Oak Park. He had plunged into the full responsibilities of his own practice, overcoming a lack of formal education and a relatively short apprenticeship and, in his words, working day and night for twenty years. His early marriage and family of six had become a burden. Mamah Borthwick Cheney, the sophisticated and artistic wife of a client, traveled with him to Europe, where he worked on the 1910 Wasmuth portfolio. The book was admired abroad and gave impetus to what later became the International style of architecture. When he returned in 1910, Frank and Catherine were unable to reconcile. Wright moved back to the land where he had derived artistic nourishment, his beloved Wisconsin farmland. There he began another home and studio, Taliesin.

To provide income for the family in Oak Park, he rented out the home and remodeled the studio into new living quarters for his family. A brick firewall was built to separate the two residences. Changes in the home were relatively minor—the front doorway was filled in, a new entry was created on the side driveway, and one of the semi-circular verandas was removed. In the living room, the north bay was replaced by a much larger alcove lined with bookshelves, and a roof was added to shelter the front porch. On the second floor of the home, the partition in the children's room was removed to make a new master bedroom.

The drafting room became a living room in 1911.

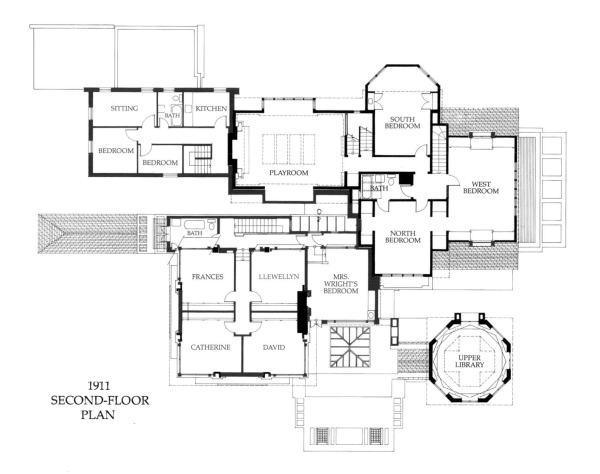

1911
SECOND-FLOOR
PLAN

The studio entry terrace was too public for a residence, and so Wright raised the wall height and made it into a private porch. He added a trellis that cantilevered over the public sidewalk. Just outside the library, he created a walled garden with a fish pond. A path led from the garden to the new dining room, which had been the office. Driveways and three garages were added; the entrance to the studio half of the new duplex was moved around to the east drive.

Inside, Wright converted the first floor of the drafting room into his family's new living room. Masking one of his greatest architectural spaces, he removed the traces of the successful studio he had worked so hard to create. Not only did he make this difficult reversal, but he did so with great care for the comfort of his family and for their aesthetic needs. For example, the arched fireplace, which worked perfectly well, was re-faced with a finer Roman brick in his more recent rectilinear style. The open balcony of the studio was floored over and the octagonal drum squared off to form four children's bedrooms. A fifth room, for Catherine, was built on the roof over the office. New trellises mingled with the branches of the ginkgo tree. Below, a canopy spanned the driveway in front of the garages. An apartment added over the garages was occupied at one time by John Lloyd Wright and his family. By 1925 the children had grown up and Catherine had moved to downtown

Chicago, and so the entire building was sold. Later it was subdivided into as many as seven different rental units, most of them with their own entrances and fireplaces.

Wright's long career had several phases in different locales and therefore exhibited somewhat different styles of architecture. After Mamah Cheney's death in 1914, he spent five years in Japan completing the Imperial Hotel. In the twenties he practiced in California, experimenting with a concrete wall construction he called "textile block." The stormy marriage to his second wife, Miriam Noel, lasted only four years. In 1928, at the age of sixty-one, he married Olgivanna Milanoff. During the Depression, they started an architectural school at Taliesin, soon expanding to a second location, Taliesin West, in the Arizona desert. Wright reached his zenith in residential design with the construction of Fallingwater in 1936. In the same year he built the first of many Usonian houses, an inexpensive, one-story residence with low lines and large areas of glass. His later works included buildings of strong geometric forms like those of his very early years, for example, the Marin County Civic Center.

Several years before his death in 1959, Wright returned to Oak Park and worked on the building for the last time. He regarded it with a mixture of nostalgia and frustration at his early architectural naïveté.

The photos on these two pages are the same view taken before, during, and after restoration. The balcony of the drafting room had been floored over to create bedrooms for Wright's children. The vertical chains and railing were removed, but the chain tension ring was imbedded in the ceiling.

After much research and analysis, the decision was made to restore the building to its appearance of 1909, the last year that Wright lived and worked here. Original materials were retained wherever possible; when removals were required, all historic features were carefully recorded or stored. Restructuring included steel reinforcement to meet modern building codes. Almost all foundations were excavated and repaired or replaced. New exterior and interior finishes and decorative arts completed the work. Every room in the studio underwent similar reconstruction. The restoration in the home was able to save more original building fabric. The project occurred over a thirteen-year period, from 1974 to 1987, cost close to $3.5 million after a climate control system was added, and involved some eighty different firms, including many specialized crafts. Volunteers contributed more than two hundred thousand work hours toward the completion of the restoration.

YE'VE LEFT A GLIMMER STILL TO CHEER
THE MAN—THE ARTIFEX·
THAT HOLDS IN SPITE O'KNOCKS AND SCALE
O'FRICTION WASTE AN SLIP
AN BY THAT LIGHT—NOW MARK MY WORD—
WE'LL BUILD THE PERFECT SHIP·

THE FRANK LLOYD WRIGHT TRUST is a Chicago-based not-for-profit organization that renews the vision of Frank Lloyd Wright through programs and educational initiatives about architecture, design and culture to perpetuate Wright's all-inclusive artistic vision and belief in the integrity of the natural and built environment.

The Trust conducts ongoing historic preservation and operates public tours, programs and events at major Wright sites, including his Home and Studio (1889/1898) in Oak Park, a Chicago suburban community; The Rookery Light Court (1905-07) in downtown Chicago; Unity Temple (1905-08) in Oak Park; the Frederick C. Robie House (1908-10) in Chicago's Hyde Park; and the Emil Bach House (1915) in Chicago's Rogers Park.

The mission of the Trust is to engage, educate and inspire the public through architecture, design and the legacy of Frank Lloyd Wright, and to preserve the Trust's historic sites and collections.

ABOVE *The studio entrance as it appeared from 1911 until 1983.*

———

OPPOSITE *Horizontal roofs and ledges like these under the great ginkgo tree were added in 1911.*

BIBLIOGRAPHY

BROOKS, H. ALLEN. *The Prairie School: Frank Lloyd Wright and His Contemporaries.* Toronto and Buffalo: University of Toronto Press, 1972.

DOWNING, ANDREW JACKSON. *The Architecture of Country Houses.* New York: Dover Publications, 1969. Originally published in 1850.

DRING, WILLIAM, THOMAS A. HEINZ, CARL J. HUNTER, DONALD G. KALEC, AND JOHN G. THORPE. *The Plan for Restoration and Adaptive Use of the Frank Lloyd Wright Home and Studio.* Chicago and London: University of Chicago Press, 1978.

EMERSON, RALPH WALDO. *Emerson's Essays.* New York: Thomas Y. Crowell & Co., 1926.

HITCHCOCK, HENRY-RUSSELL. *In the Nature of Materials, 1887–1941: The Buildings of Frank Lloyd Wright.* New York: Horizon Press, 1973.

KAKUZO, OKAKURA. *The Book of Tea.* Rutland, Vt., and Tokyo: Charles E. Tuttle Co., 1956. Originally published in 1906.

MANSON, GRANT CARPENTER. *Frank Lloyd Wright to 1910: The First Golden Age.* New York: Reinhold, 1958.

MEEHAN, PATRICK J., ed. *The Master Architect: Conversations with Frank Lloyd Wright.* New York: John Wiley & Sons, 1984.

MORSE, EDWARD S. *Japanese Homes and Their Surroundings.* New York: Dover Publications, 1961. Originally published in 1886.

SCULLY, VINCENT, JR. *Frank Lloyd Wright.* Masters of World Architecture series. New York: George Braziller, 1960.

SCULLY, VINCENT, JR. *The Shingle Style Today.* New York: George Braziller, 1974.

SMITH, NORRIS KELLY. *Frank Lloyd Wright: A Study in Architectural Content.* Watkins Glen, N.Y.: American Life Foundation, 1979.

STORRER, WILLIAM ALLIN. *The Architecture of Frank Lloyd Wright: A Complete Catalog.* Cambridge, Mass., and London: MIT Press, 1978.

SULLIVAN, LOUIS H. *The Autobiography of an Idea.* New York: Dover Publications, 1956. Originally published in 1924.

TWOMBLY, ROBERT C. *Frank Lloyd Wright: His Life and His Architecture.* New York: John Wiley & Sons, 1979.

WHITMAN, WALT. *The Complete Poetry of Walt Whitman.* American Classics series. New York: Pellegrini & Cudahy, 1948.

WRIGHT, FRANK LLOYD. *An Autobiography.* New York: Horizon Press, 1977.

WRIGHT, FRANK LLOYD. *Drawings and Plans of Frank Lloyd Wright: The Early Period (1893–1909).* New York: Dover Publications, 1983. Originally published in 1910 by Ernst Wasmuth, Berlin.

WRIGHT, FRANK LLOYD. *The Early Work of Frank Lloyd Wright.* New York: Dover Publications, 1982. Originally published in 1911 by Ernst Wasmuth, Berlin.

WRIGHT, FRANK LLOYD. *The Natural House.* New York: Horizon Press, 1982.

WRIGHT, FRANK LLOYD. *Frank Lloyd Wright: Writings and Buildings.* Selected by Edgar Kaufmann, Jr., and Ben Raeburn. New York: New American Library, 1974.

WRIGHT, JOHN LLOYD. *My Father Who Is on Earth.* New York: G. P. Putnam's Sons, 1946.

Text and design: ANN ABERNATHY, AIA, has taught architectural design at MIT and at the School of the Art Institute of Chicago. From 1982 to 1987, she was a restoration architect at the Frank Lloyd Wright Trust.

Design and editing: JOHN G. THORPE, AIA, is an architect who served the Trust as a charter board member, president and vice president in charge of the restoration program.

This publication was originally made possible through funding from the Sears Family of companies.

The Frank Lloyd Wright Trust would like to express gratitude to David and Gladys Wright, Donald Kalec, Joseph Alderfer, Dean Eckenfels, and the Oak Park Conservatory.

Frank Lloyd Wright Trust
209 S. LaSalle Street, Chicago, Illinois 60604

flwright.org

shopwright.org

travelwright.org

ILLUSTRATION CREDITS

ANN ABERNATHY, 19, 29, 31, 32, 33 top, 33 bottom, 37 top, 40, 44 bottom, 48
JUDITH BROMLEY, 8, 11, 12, 14, 15, 17 top, 20 bottom, 22 bottom, 23 top
CHESTER BRUMMEL, 2, 13, 18 left, 20 top, 20 center, 22 top, 26, 34, 41
HENRY FUERMANN, 42 bottom
HENRY-RUSSELL HITCHCOCK, 4
House Beautiful, 5 bottom, 6 top
PETER JOHNSEN, 39
DONALD G. KALEC, Cover, 30, 38 top, 44 top, 46
JON MILLER, HEDRICH-BLESSING, 16, 18 right, 21, 24-25, 27, 35, 36, 38 bottom, 45
JOHN THORPE, 47
ANN WILLIAMSEN, 3, 33 center, 37 bottom
FRANK LLOYD WRIGHT FOUNDATION, Inside front cover, 5 bottom, 6 bottom, 10
FRANK LLOYD WRIGHT TRUST, 5 top left and right, 9, 23 bottom, all plans.

Other publications by the Frank Lloyd Wright Trust:

Frank Lloyd Wright's Robie House, 2010
Hometown Architect: The Complete Buildings of Frank Lloyd Wright in Oak Park and River Forest, Illinois, 2006
Building a Legacy: The Restoration of Frank Lloyd Wright's Oak Park Home and Studio, 2001
Frank Lloyd Wright and the Prairie, 1998
In Wright's Shadow: Artists and Architects at the Oak Park Studio, 1998